A TO Z

GUIDE TO

HORSES & PONIES

by Randi Hacker

Scholastic Inc.

New York   Toronto   London   Auckland   Sydney
Mexico City   New Delhi   Hong Kong

ISBN 0-439-07054-6

12 11 10 9 8 7 6 5 4 3 2   9/9 0 1 2 3 4/0

Printed in the U.S.A.   01

First Scholastic printing, March 1999

Dear Reader,

Welcome to *Your A to Z Guide to Horses and Ponies*. There's a lot for you to know and learn about horses and ponies and you'll find plenty of information in these pages. From Andalusian to Zweibrucker, from arena to yearling, this *A to Z Guide* is packed with facts and pictures all related to your favorite four-hoofed friends.

And this guide is conveniently cross-referenced; that means if you come across a word that's bold-faced within a definition, you can look that word up in this book, too!

Love,

The Editors

Action—The way
a horse moves. For
example, high-knee
action is very showy.

Aids—Any signals riders or drivers give horses
and ponies to let them know what they want
them to do. For example, when you nudge a
horse's sides with your heels, your heels are an
aid to ask the horse to go faster. When you pull
up on the **reins**, your hands are an aid to ask
the horse to slow down.

Airs Above the Ground—Spectacular moves
done by specially trained horses in which their
legs come off the ground and maneuvers are
performed in the air. See also **Capriole**,
Courbette, and **Levade**.

Albino—Any horse that has pink skin and white
hair. Some albinos have red eyes. Others have
pale blue eyes known as **glass eyes**.

Anatomy—Science that deals with the parts of the body. Here's a diagram of a horse's anatomy:

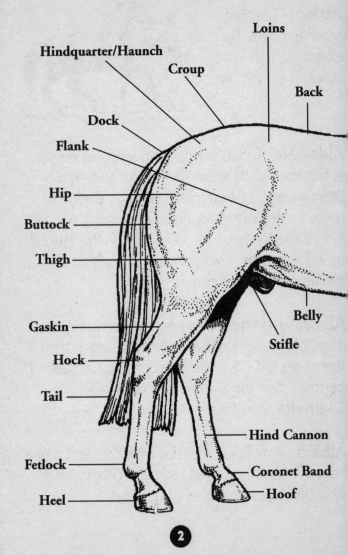

Loins

Hindquarter/Haunch

Croup

Back

Dock

Flank

Hip

Buttock

Thigh

Belly

Stifle

Gaskin

Hock

Tail

Hind Cannon

Fetlock

Coronet Band

Heel

Hoof

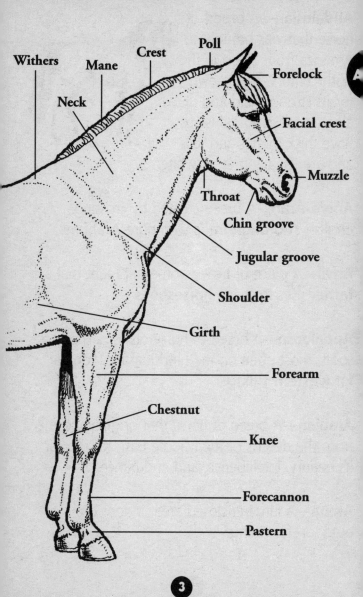

Withers

Crest

Poll

Mane

Forelock

Neck

Facial crest

Muzzle

Throat

Chin groove

Jugular groove

Shoulder

Girth

Forearm

Chestnut

Knee

Forecannon

Pastern

Andalusian—A **breed** of horse that was brought to America from Spain in the 16th century. It is known for its strong build and elegant looks. Andalusians have thick manes and tails and are usually gray or white.

Anglo-Arab—A breed created by crossing English **Thoroughbreds** with pure **Arabians**.

Anvil—A piece of heavy iron equipment that a **farrier** uses to shape **horseshoes**.

Appaloosa—A breed of horse distinguished by spots, most often on the hindquarters. Popular for **western riding**.

Arabian—A breed of horse that originally came from the deserts of the Middle East. Known for its beauty, intelligence, and endurance.

Arena—A large enclosed area, indoor or outdoor, for riding.

Backing—A move in which a pony or horse is given a signal by its rider to take a few steps backward.

Bald Face—White **markings** that cover the entire front of a horse's or pony's face.

Barrel—The part of a horse right under the **saddle**.

Bay—Horses or ponies with dark brown coats and black **points** (mane, tail, lower legs).

Belgian—Type of **draft horse** that is strong, heavy, and can weigh more than 2,000 pounds. One of the largest breed of horses.

Binocular—Seeing the same view with both eyes. Because horses' and ponies' eyes are on the sides of their heads, they are only binocular when they look forward. See **Monocular**.

Bit—The part of the **bridle** that goes into the horse's or pony's mouth. See illustration under **Bridle**.

Blaze—A broad white marking that covers most of a horse's or pony's forehead and can extend down to its muzzle.

Blinkers—Device attached to a bridle that prevents a horse or pony from looking anywhere but forward. Also called blinders.

Bolt—What a horse or pony does when it panics and runs.

Boots—Footgear worn by a person while riding. There are English boots and western boots. English boots are tall leather boots with a rounded toe, low heel, and laces. Western boots are ornamented and have a pointy toe and a higher heel (they are also called cowboy boots).

Box Stall—A large room in a stable where a horse or pony can move about freely.

Breed—A group of horses or ponies that look alike and come from a common ancestor.

Bridle—1. Noun: Leather headgear for horses and ponies. 2. Verb: To put a bridle on.

Bridle

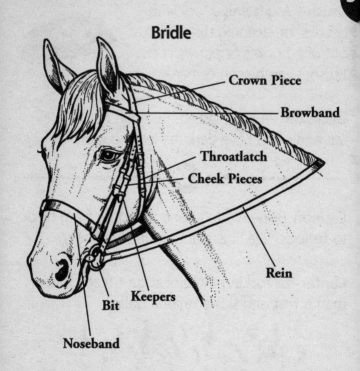

Crown Piece

Browband

Throatlatch

Cheek Pieces

Rein

Keepers

Bit

Noseband

Bridle Path—1. A trail for riding. 2. A portion of the **mane** just behind the ears that is clipped to make it easier to put the bridle on.

Browband—The part of the bridle that comes across a horse's or pony's forehead above his eyes. See illustration under **Bridle**.

Brush—A grooming tool with bristles for cleaning dirt and dust out of a horse's or pony's coat. Brushes can be soft or hard.

Buckskin—A color breed. Buckskin horses are tan and often have dark manes and tails.

C

Cannon Bone—A leg bone that goes from **hock** to **fetlock**. See illustration under **Anatomy**.

Canter—A rocking three-beat **gait** that's faster than a **trot** and slower than a **gallop**.

Cantle—The high back part of the **saddle**. See illustration under **Saddle**.

Capriole—An airs-above-the-ground move in which a horse jumps off all four legs into the air, then kicks with his back legs while airborne.

Carriage Horse—Any horse that pulls a carriage. Many different breeds can be carriage horses.

Centaur—A creature from Greek mythology that is half horse, half human.

Cheek Piece—The part of the bridle that runs down the horse's or pony's cheeks. The bit is attached to it. See illustration under **Bridle**.

Chestnut—1. Noun: A horny growth on the inside of a horse's knee. 2. Adj.: A reddish-brown color for horses or ponies—coat, mane, and tail are all this color.

Clydesdale—A heavy, tall draft horse breed from Scotland. Clydesdales are known for the **feathery** hair on their legs. Long ago, these horses carried knights in armor.

Cob—A short-legged, strong, small horse.

Color Breed—Horses and ponies that are identified by their color patterns.

Colt—A male **foal** (baby horse or pony).

Connemara Pony—Small, strong breed from Ireland that makes an excellent riding pony.

Contact—The connection between the rider's hands and the pony's mouth through the reins. This term is used in **English riding**, not western.

Coronet Band—The place at the top of a horse's or pony's hoof where it meets the skin of the leg. See illustration under **Anatomy**.

Courbette—An **airs-above-the-ground** move in which the horse rears up, then does a series of hops on its hind legs.

Croup—The part of the horse just above its tail. See illustration under **Anatomy**.

Crown Piece—The part of the bridle that goes over the top of the horse's or pony's head and behind the ears. See illustration under **Bridle**.

Curb Chain—A chain under the bit that is used to guide and help control a horse or pony.

Curry Comb—A hard, usually plastic, grooming tool used to break up clumps of mud and dislodge dirt from a horse's or pony's coat. Also used to clean hair and dust out of **brushes**.

— D —

Dapples—Spots of the same color in a horse's or pony's coat. The spots indicate good health.

Dapple Gray—A color pattern for a horse or pony—gray with darker gray spots.

Darley Arabian—One of the very first Arabian horses in history, the Darley Arabian is an ancestor of the present-day Thoroughbred breed.

Dartmoor Pony—Rugged, small pony from Dartmoor, in England. Known as a fine children's mount.

Dished Face—A type of horse or pony face that curves slightly inward between the forehead and nose. Arabians are known for their dish faces.

Dock—The bony part at the base of a horse's or pony's tail. See illustration under **Anatomy**.

Draft Horse—The heaviest and biggest type of horse. Draft horses are used for all kinds of pulling, including logging and plowing. **Belgians**, **Percherons**, and **Clydesdales** are all draft horses.

Dressage (dress-AHJ)—A type of riding in which horses perform complicated moves without the use of noticeable aids from the rider. When riding dressage, horse and rider move together as one.

Dun—A horse with a yellowish- or grayish-brown coat, and legs, mane, and tail that are black; it occasionally has a dark stripe down its back. Duns can also have zebralike stripes on their legs.

E

English Riding—One of two different styles of riding. The other is **western riding**. English riders use both hands on the reins, a short **stirrup**, and a small saddle.

Eohippus—The very first horse on earth, eohippus lived 40–55 million years ago. Its name means "dawn horse," and at 10–17 inches tall, it was no bigger than a fox.

Equestrian—1. Noun: One who rides on horseback. 2. Adj.: Relating to, or featuring horseback riding.

Equilibrium—Balance. It is something that is very important to have in order to be a good rider.

Exmoor Pony—A very ancient breed of pony living half wild in the area of Exmoor, in England.

F

Falabella Pony—A tiny breed of pony with an average height of 28 to 31 inches. They are bred in Argentina from Shetland ponies.

Farrier—A person who takes care of horses' and ponies' hooves. Farriers trim hooves when they grow too long. They also put on horseshoes.

Feather—Long, silky hair that grows on the fetlock of some horses and ponies.

Feral Horses—Domestic horses that have become wild. This includes almost all wild horses today.

Fetlock—The round joint at the back of horses' and ponies' legs just above the hoof. Tufts of hair often grow here. See illustration under **Anatomy**.

Filly—A female **foal** (baby horse or pony).

Flea-bitten—A color pattern in which there are small patches of reddish hair.

Foal—1. Noun: A baby horse. 2. Verb: To give birth to a baby horse.

Forelock—The tuft of hair that falls over a horse's or pony's forehead.

Founder—A painful foot condition that is caused by overeating. Ponies are especially prone to founder. If your pony is overweight and limping, call a vet right away. To prevent founder, limit your pony's diet.

Friesian—An ancient Dutch breed of horse.

Frog—The v-shaped soft pad on the bottom of a horse's or pony's foot.

Gaits—The speeds at which horses and ponies move. There are four basic gaits: **walk, trot, canter, gallop**.

Gallop—The fastest of the four horse and pony gaits.

Galloway Pony—Large, fast, and now extinct, this Scottish pony was one of the ancestors of today's Thoroughbred.

Gelding—A neutered male horse.

Girth—1. The part of the horse or pony just behind its front legs. See illustration under **Anatomy**. 2. A belt that keeps the saddle on the horse or pony. It buckles onto one side of the saddle, passes under the animal, and buckles onto the other side.

Glass Eyes—Pale blue eyes found in **albino** horses as well as in some **dappled** horses.

Grass Belly—A very rounded belly that comes from eating too much raw food. Often found in ponies.

Graze—To move around in a field and eat grass.

Green—Used to describe a horse that is tame enough to be ridden but isn't yet trained.

Grey—A horse or pony with white hair on darker skin. Greys are born dark and turn gray or white when they are about eight years old.

Groom—1. Noun: The person in charge of keeping horses or ponies. 2. Verb: To clean and brush a horse or pony.

H

Hackamore—A bridle that doesn't use a bit but instead has a rope loop to hold it on the horse's or pony's nose.

G H

Haflinger—A small-sized mountain breed of horse from the Tyrol area in Austria.

Halter—Headgear for a horse or pony, usually made of rope, cotton, or nylon. It has no bit.

Hand—The unit of measurement for a horse's or pony's height. One hand equals 4 inches.

Hanoverian—A large breed of **saddle horse** particularly good at jumping.

Harness—Equipment used to attach horses and ponies to carts and plows.

Haunches—The hindquarters of a horse or pony. See illustration under **Anatomy**.

Hay—Dried grass fed to horses or ponies mostly during the winter when fresh grass is scarce.

Helmet—A hard hat worn to protect the rider's head while riding.

Highland Pony—A breed of large pony that comes from Scotland.

Hippology—The science of horses. From the Greek *hippus*, meaning "horse."

Hock—A joint in the rear leg. It bends toward the back. See illustration under **Anatomy**.

Hoof—The horny, hard part of a horse's or pony's foot. See illustration under **Anatomy**.

Hoofpick—An instrument used to clean dirt and stones out of a horse's or pony's hoof.

Horse—A horse is an **ungulate**, which means it has hooves and eats plants. Horses stand 14.2 hands or taller.

Horseshoe—A curved piece of metal the same shape as a horse's or pony's hoof that is nailed into the hoof to protect it from wear.

Icelandic Pony—Small, strong, and hardy breed from Iceland. Known for its fast, comfortable gait called **tolting**.

In and Out—A type of jump consisting of two jumps in a row with as little as one stride between them.

Indian Pony—A small, hardy breed whose ancestors were brought to America from Spain hundreds of years ago. **Appaloosas** are a type of Indian pony.

Irish Hunter—A breed of horse that is half Thoroughbred. Known for its outstanding jumping ability.

Isabella—A yellowish-brown, golden yellow, chestnut, bay, or gray horse that has a light mane and tail. Golden Isabellas are called **palominos**.

J

Jockey—A person who rides or drives a horse especially as a professional in a race.

Jodhpurs—Riding trousers. The legs fit tightly from the calf to the ankle. The seat is wide and roomy. They are worn with short boots. Originated in India.

Jumper—A horse trained to jump.

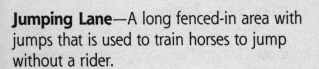

Jumping Lane—A long fenced-in area with jumps that is used to train horses to jump without a rider.

Jutland—A medium-sized breed of horse from Denmark.

J

K

Kabachi—A Russian sport using horses in which riders gallop past a ring mounted on a post and try to toss a spear through it.

Kabardin—A breed of horse from Russia.

Karabakh—A rare breed of horse from Azerbaijan (part of what used to be the Soviet Union). This breed is small and temperamental.

Kazakh (ka-ZAK)—A tough, hardy breed that is approximately 2,000 years old. These horses are from the lower reaches of the Volga River in Russia and are popular with Mongolian riders.

Keeper—A small leather band that keeps the ends of the bridle straps from flapping around. See illustration under **Bridle**.

Khis-kouhou—Mongolian horse sport meaning "bride hunt." Young men on horses ride after girls, also on horses, and try to kiss them.

Kicking—What horses and ponies do to defend themselves. They do this by thrusting their hind legs out backward.

Knee Roll—The padded part of the saddle flaps that are designed to support the rider's knee. See illustration under **Saddle**.

L

Lame—What a horse or pony is called when it has a foot injury that prevents it from walking comfortably.

Large-animal Veterinarians—Animal doctors that tend to large animals such as horses.

Lead—When a person holds onto a horse's or pony's bridle and guides it to walk beside him or her.

Lead Rope—A rope with a hook on one end that attaches to the halter. Used to lead a horse or pony from one place to another and to tie it up.

Leg Wrap—A soft bandage-like strip of cloth that is wound around the lower leg of a horse or pony. Leg wraps come in different colors and are used for decoration as well as for support and warmth.

Levade (luh-VAHD)— An airs-above-the-ground move in which the horse rears up and balances on its hind legs.

Lipizzaner—A breed of horse bred on a farm called Lipizza, in Slovenia. Lipizzaner stallions were once used by Austrian royalty as war horses. They

are famous for their **airs above the ground**. They are born with dark coats that become white by the time they are ten years old. One out of a hundred Lipizzaners never turns white.

Lunge (or Longe) Rein—A long rein that attaches to the halter and is used to make a horse or pony go around the trainer in a large circle.

Mane—The long hair that grows on the back of a horse's or pony's neck. See illustration under **Anatomy**.

Mane Comb—A comb used to groom the mane of a horse or pony.

Mare—A female horse or pony.

Markings—The white patches on a horse's or pony's head or legs. The markings help make it possible to tell horses or ponies apart from others of the same breed or color.

Martingale—A leather device that prevents a horse or pony from rearing or throwing its head too high. It attaches to the bridle and girth.

Monocular—Seeing two different views, one with each eye. Horses and ponies are monocular when looking from side to side or backward because their eyes are set on the sides of their heads.

Morgan—This small, hardy breed of horse or pony is the state breed of Vermont. This breed is descended from a stallion called Justin Morgan, born in 1789.

Mustang—A wild horse of Spanish origin found in the western United States.

Muzzle—The horse's or pony's nose and mouth. See illustration under **Anatomy**.

N

Neck Reining—In western riding, the way a rider uses her hands and reins to tell the horse which way to turn.

New Forest Pony—A half-wild breed that lives in the New Forest in the southwest of England.

Nicker—A friendly low sound made by a horse or pony that is happy to see you.

Noble—Arab and English purebred horses and ponies are called nobles.

Nosebag—A canvas bag filled with feed that hangs from a horse's or pony's head, covering its mouth. Horses and ponies eat from it.

Noseband—That part of the bridle that goes around the nose. See illustration under **Bridle**.

Norwegian Fjord Pony—A large, strong breed from Norway with an unusual mane: The outer hairs are white and the inner hairs are black, so the mane is striped white, black, and white.

Oldenburg—Breed of horse originally used to pull carriages, now used as a **saddle horse**.

Overreach—When the hind foot hits the forefoot as the horse or pony moves.

OX—These two letters are written after the name of an Arabian to indicate that it is purebred.

Oxer—A high, widespread fence used in show jumping.

P

Paint Horse—**Piebald** or **skewbald** horses of Thoroughbred or **quarter horse** breeds.

Palomino—Known as the Golden Horse. This color breed is identified by its golden coat and white mane and tail.

Pastern—The part of a horse's or pony's foot from the fetlock to the hoof. See illustration under **Anatomy**.

Pasture—A field with grass where horses and ponies graze.

Percheron—This breed is a powerful draft horse originally from France.

Piebald—A color pattern in which the coat has black and white patches or markings.

Pinto—A piebald horse of any breed other than Thoroughbred or quarter horse.

Points—What a horse's or pony's legs, mane, and tail are referred to in a discussion of visual characteristics. For example, a bay is brown with black points (legs, mane, and tail).

Poll—The top of a horse's or pony's head. See illustration under **Anatomy**.

Pommel—The front part of the saddle. See illustration under **Saddle** (English Saddle).

Pony—A pony is an ungulate, which means it has hooves and eats plants. Ponies measure 14.2 hands and smaller.

O
P

Posting Trot—A fast trot during which the rider rises and sits in rhythm with the horse's or pony's leg movements.

Przewalski's (shuh-VAL-skee)—The last wild horse breed still in existence. Small, stocky, and dun-colored with a short, erect mane. It's found in Central Asia.

—◆—**Q**—◆—

Quadriga (KWAD-ri-ga)—A type of carriage used in Ancient Greece and Rome, which was drawn by four horses standing side by side.

Quadrille (kwa-DRIL)—A dance that horses are trained to do to music. This dance is done by groups of eight or twelve horses.

Quarter Horse—A breed of horse known for the great speed it can reach over a quarter-mile distance. Quarter horses are also called quarter milers and are very muscular.

Quarters—Any part of a horse's or pony's body that is behind its chest.

Racehorse—A horse bred for its speed and endurance. The **Thoroughbred** is the best example of a racehorse.

Rear—A move in which a horse or pony rises on its hind legs. Horses and ponies may rear when they are startled or angry.

P Q R

Reins—Long leather straps on the bridle that extend from the bit to the rider's hands. Reins are used to control the horse's or pony's movements. See illustration under **Bridle**.

Roan—A description of any horse's or pony's coat that has white hairs mixed in.

Run-in Shelter—A structure in a pasture that a horse or pony can enter and leave on its own for protection from the weather.

Saddle—The piece of tack a rider sits on. There are different types of saddles, including English, western, dressage, and Australian.

English Saddle

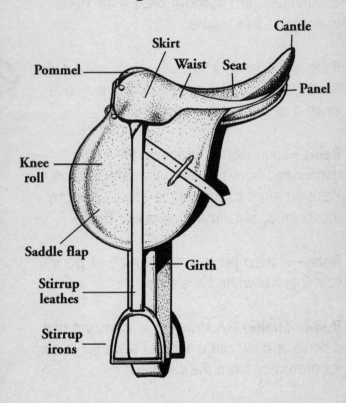

Pommel · Skirt · Waist · Seat · Cantle · Panel · Knee roll · Saddle flap · Girth · Stirrup leathes · Stirrup irons

Western Saddle

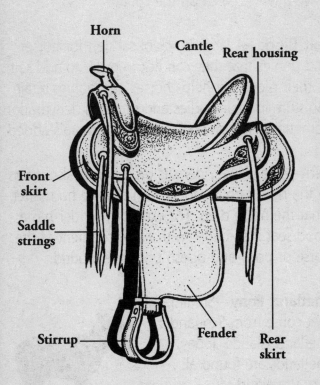

Horn

Cantle

Rear housing

Front
skirt

Saddle
strings

Stirrup

Fender

Rear
skirt

Saddle Horse—A horse that is trained to be ridden.

Saddle Sore—A skin infection horses and ponies get that is caused by a saddle that doesn't fit well. Saddle sores can take a long time to heal and can leave a white patch on the coat.

Salt Block—A large block of salt left for horses and ponies that they can lick in order to add salt to their diets. Salt helps horses and ponies retain moisture in their bodies and prevents dehydration. Sometimes salt blocks have other minerals added.

Seat—The way a rider sits on a horse. Also refers to the rider's ability to stay on a horse no matter what the horse does. For example, a rider has a good seat if she rides with the movement of the horse or pony and doesn't bounce around.

Shetland Pony—Small ponies that come from Scotland's Shetland Islands. Today, Shetlands are found all over the world.

Shire—The world's largest breed of horse, originally from England. Some stallions can be six feet tall (18 hands) at the withers and weigh as much as 2,500 pounds.

Shoe—1. Noun: A curved piece of metal nailed to a horse's or pony's hoof. 2. Verb: To put a shoe on a horse or pony.

Shy—When a horse or pony is said to shy it means it swerves to one side suddenly. Usually this is because it's startled or scared by something.

Single-toed—All members of the horse family, including ponies, have only one toe.

Sire—1. Noun: The father of a line of horses. 2. Verb: To father a line of horses.

Sitting Trot—A slow-paced trot during which the rider sits in the saddle without bouncing or rising.

Skewbald—A color pattern in which the horse's or pony's coat has patches of white and any other color except black.

Snip—A small white marking between the nostrils and upper lip.

Sorrell—A light **chestnut**-colored horse that usually has a white mane and tail.

Sound—A horse or pony that is healthy.

Stallion—A male horse.

Standing Stall—A compartment in which a horse or pony is kept tied standing up.

Star—A white marking on a horse's or pony's forehead.

Steeplechase—A horse race in which the horses must jump many obstacles. The winner is the horse that clears the greatest number of obstacles in the shortest time.

tifle—The joint above the hock in a horse's or pony's hind leg. See illustration under **Anatomy**.

tirrup—A metal or wooden device attached to the saddle into which the rider puts her foot. See illustration under **Saddle**.

trangles—A contagious disease of horses and ponies that causes a high fever and a swelling of the glands under the jaw. It takes a few weeks for infected animals to recover.

traw—Dried wheat or other types of grass used for bedding in a stall. It's not for eating.

tripe—A thin white line down the middle of a horse's or pony's face.

S

tud—A stallion that's kept specifically for breeding with other horses.

Swayback—A horse or pony whose back is sagging. It can be hereditary or caused by a heavy rider. Mares who have had many foals are often swaybacked.

Sweat Scraper—A metal tool used to remove sweat or water from a horse's or pony's body.

T

Tack—Equipment used in riding and driving horses and ponies, including saddles and bridles.

Team—Horses or ponies that are harnessed together for the purpose of pulling a vehicle.

Thoroughbred—A horse and pony breed known for its speed. It's descended from three Arabian stallions that lived in the early 1700s.

Throatlatch—A loosely buckled strip of leather on a bridle that passes under the horse's or pony's throat. Used to keep the bridle on the animal's face. See illustration under **Bridle**.

Thrush—A disease that affects horses' and ponies' feet. It's caused by a fungus and can be treated.

Tolting—A fast, comfortable gait. It's the natural gait of Icelandic ponies and can be taught to other pony breeds.

Trakehner (tra-KAY-ner)—A saddle horse breed that originated in Prussia in the 18th century.

Trot—A two-beat gait. It's the second slowest gait, walking being the slowest.

Two-point Position—An action in which the rider rises in the stirrups and leans forward. Used for jumping or when riding at a gallop.

U

Ukrainian Warm-blood—A breed of horse that's a combination of mixed **Thoroughbred**, **Trakehner**, and **Hanoverian** bloodlines.

Ungulate—A type or group of mammals that has four legs, hooves, and eats plants. Horses and ponies are members of this group.

Unharness—To take the harness off.

Unhitch—To unfasten a horse or pony from a cart or other vehicle.

Unsound—A horse or pony that's not healthy.

Upright Mane—A mane that falls down both sides of the neck as opposed to falling on one side.

V

Vaccinate—To inoculate against disease. Horses and ponies should be vaccinated in the spring against rabies, tetanus, and other diseases.

Vaquero (vah-CARE-oh)—A Spanish word, it's what Mexican cowboys are called.

Vaulting—The act of performing gymnastics on a horse while it moves.

Victoria—An open horse-drawn carriage with four wheels that carries two people. It has a folding hood.

Volte (vole-TAY)—A dressage move in which the horse does a full turn on its **haunches**.

W

Walk—The slowest of the four gaits.

War Horse—A strong and agile horse that carried knights in armor into battle long ago.

Welsh Pony—A breed that comes from Wales, now found all over the world. These ponies are good jumpers.

Western Riding—One of two different types of riding. The other is **English riding**. Western riders use a big saddle with a horn, long stirrups, and a neck rein.

Whinny—A loud horse-and-pony call that carries a long distance.

White Muzzle—A physical characteristic of a horse or pony in which white markings cover both lips up to the nostrils.

White Stocking—A physical characteristic of a horse or pony in which white markings extend up to or over the ankle joint.

Winkers—Another name for **blinkers**.

Withers—The highest part of a horse's or pony's back at the base of the neck between the shoulder blades. This is the place at which a horse's or pony's height is measured. See illustration under **Anatomy**.

X—An X after a horse's name indicates that it is a purebred Anglo-Arab. This means all its ancestors were English Thoroughbreds or purebred Arabians.

XX—Placed after a horse's name it means that the horse is an English Thoroughbred.

Xenophon (ZEE-na-fon)—An ancient Greek author who lived from about 430 BC to 354 BC. He wrote the first book on the art of classical riding. Some of his ideas are still used today.

Yearling—Any horse or pony that is one year old.

Yoke—The wooden bar joining two draft animals together in order to make a work team to pull a vehicle like a plow or a carriage.

Yorkshire Coach Horse—A breed of carriage horse with a high percentage of Thoroughbred blood. It's an excellent riding horse.

Z

Zweibrucker (TSVI-brooker)—A breed of horse from Pfalz, in Germany.